Thérèse

J

Prayer Book

FAMILY PUBLICATIONS · OXFORD

ISBN 978-1-871217-85-8

published by
Family Publications
Denis Riches House
66 Sandford Lane, Kennington
Oxford, OX1 5RP
www.familypublications.co.uk

printed in England
through s|s|media ltd

Table of Contents

Thérèse Martin was born in Normandy in 1873 and at an early age entered the Carmelite convent of Lisieux, where she became *Sister Thérèse of the Child Jesus and of the Holy Face*. She died of tuberculosis on 30 September 1897, aged 24. She was canonised in 1925 by Pope Pius XI, and declared a Patroness of the Missions in 1927. In 1997 she was declared a Doctor of the Church by Pope John Paul II. Her feast day is 1 October. She is now one of our most popular saints.

"St Thérèse of Lisieux, who never left her Carmel, through contemplative prayer and the correspondence she maintained with priests ... lived an authentic missionary spirit in her own way, accompanying every person in her Gospel service and giving the world a new spiritual orientation.

I therefore hope that the celebrations taking place ... will strengthen the mission awareness of the baptised ... through prayer, witness of life and Christian commitment in all its forms, so that every member of the faithful may be a missionary where he or she lives. I also hope for the birth of vocations to proclaim the Gospel to people who do not yet know it."

Pope Benedict XVI
12 September 2007

Introduction

The relics of St Thérèse of Lisieux are to visit Britain for the first time, from 16 September to 7 October 2009. This prayer book will help people to prepare for the visit, to understand the life and spirituality of this saint, to pray, and to find their way to God, whether on pilgrimage or at home.

Before her death in 1897, St Thérèse expressed the desire to work as a missionary, spreading the faith to distant parts of the world. Whilst her early death prevented the fulfilment of this ambition, over the last fifteen years her relics have travelled to many countries, inspiring thousands of pilgrims to pray in their presence.

St Thérèse died in relative obscurity, but over the years her teaching has steadily grown in influence and in popularity. Yet Thérèse never wrote a book on theology; instead, her teaching consists in her call to universal holiness, prayer, and evangelisation, as well as her profound sense of what it means to have a vocation. Her life serves as a model of charity, and, together with her sisters and parents, as an example for families everywhere.

In this booklet, passages from her writings are accompanied by prayers – both by and to St Thérèse – because as the saint herself demonstrates, prayer is the most fundamental form of theology. Anyone seeking to know St Thérèse and her message for the Church, or to increase their devotion to this, "the greatest saint of modern times", will find great riches within.

Saint Thérèse Doctor of the Church

Pope John Paul II

Some circumstances contribute to making her designation as a Teacher for the Church of our time even more significant.

First of all, Thérèse is a woman, who in approaching the Gospel knew how to grasp its hidden wealth with that practicality and deep resonance of life and wisdom which belong to the feminine genius. Because of her universality she stands out among the multitude of holy women who are resplendent for their Gospel wisdom.

Thérèse is also a contemplative. In the hiddenness of her Carmel she lived the great adventure of Christian experience to the point of knowing the breadth, length, height and depth of Christ's love (cf. Eph 3:18-19). God did not want his secrets to remain hidden, but enabled Thérèse to proclaim the secrets of the King (cf. MS C, 2 vo). By her life Thérèse offers a witness and theological illustration of the beauty of the contemplative life as the total dedication to Christ, Spouse of the Church, and as an affirmation of God's primacy over all things. Hers is a hidden life which possesses a mysterious fruitfulness for spreading the Gospel and fills the Church and the world with the sweet odour of Christ (cf. LT 169, 2 vo).

Lastly, Thérèse of Lisieux is a young person. She reached the maturity of holiness in the prime of youth (cf. MS C, 4 ro). As such, she appears as a Teacher of evangelical life, particularly effective in illumining the paths of young people, who must be the leaders and witnesses of the Gospel to the new generations.

Thérèse of the Child Jesus is not only the youngest Doctor of the Church, but is also the closest to us in time, as if to emphasize the continuity with which the Spirit of the Lord sends his messengers to the Church, men and women as teachers and witnesses to the faith. In fact, whatever changes can be noted in the course of history and despite the repercussions they usually have on the life and thought of individuals in every age, we must never lose sight of the continuity which links the Doctors of the Church to each other: in every historical context they remain witnesses to the unchanging Gospel and, with the light and strength that come from the Holy Spirit, they become its messengers, returning to proclaim it in its purity to their contemporaries. Thérèse is a Teacher for our time, which thirsts for living and essential words, for heroic and credible acts of witness. For this reason she is also loved and accepted by brothers and sisters of other Christian communities and even by non-Christians.

Divini Amoris Scientia 11
19 October 1997

Les Buissonnets, Thérèse's family home in Lisieux.

" I ask Jesus to draw me into the flames of His love, to unite me so closely to Him that He live and act in me. "

Surrounded with love

God was pleased all through my life to surround me with *love*, and the first memories I have are stamped with smiles and the most tender caresses. But although He placed so much *love* near me, He also sent much love into my little heart, making it warm and affectionate. I loved Mama and Papa very much and showed my tenderness for them in a thousand ways, for I was very expressive.

MS A 4 vo

O Jesus! ... I come to you with confidence, recalling that "those who are well do not need a doctor but the sick do." I beg you, then, to cure me and to pardon me. I will keep in mind, Lord, "that the soul to whom you have forgiven more should also love you more than the others"!... I offer you every beat of my heart as so many acts of love and reparation and I unite them to your infinite merits. I beg you, O my Divine Bridegroom, to be the Restorer of my soul, to act in me despite my resistance; and lastly, I wish to have no other will but yours. Tomorrow, with the help of your grace, I will begin a new life in which each moment will be an act of love and renunciation.

Amen.

Prayer 7

Praying as a child

One day, one of my teachers at the Abbey asked me what I did on my free afternoons when I was alone. I told her I went behind my bed in an empty space which was there, and that it was easy to close myself in with my bedcurtain and that "I *thought*." "But what do you *think* about?" she asked. "I think about God, about life, about Eternity ... I *think*!" The good religious laughed heartily at me, and later on she loved reminding me of the time when I *thought*, asking me if I *was still thinking*. I understand now that I was making mental prayer without knowing it and that God was already instructing me in secret.

MS A 33 vo

O Lord,

You said: "Unless you become as little children, you shall not enter into the kingdom of heaven." Grant us so to follow in humility and simplicity of heart the footsteps of the virgin Thérèse that we may obtain everlasting reward as your adopted children.

Amen.

Our Lady of the Smile. Thérèse, when critically ill as a child, was healed while praying before this statue.

Why I love you O Mary

Mother full of grace, I know that in Nazareth
You live in poverty, wanting nothing more.
No rapture, miracle, or ecstasy
Embellish your life, O Queen of the Elect!
The number of little ones on earth is truly great.
They can raise their eyes to you without trembling.
It's by the ordinary way, incomparable Mother,
That you like to walk to guide them to Heaven.

While waiting for Heaven, O my dear Mother,
I want to live with you, to follow you each day.
Mother, contemplating you, I joyfully immerse myself,
Discovering in your heart abysses of love.
Your motherly gaze banishes all my fears.
It teaches me to cry, it teaches me to rejoice.
Instead of scorning pure and simple joys,
You want to share in them, you deign to bless them.

Soon I'll hear that sweet harmony.
Soon I'll go to beautiful Heaven to see you.
You who came to smile at me in the morning of my life,
Come smile at me again … Mother … It's evening now!
I no longer fear the splendour of your supreme glory.
With you I've suffered and now I want
To sing on your lap, Mary, why I love you,
And to go on saying that I am your child!

Poem 54 stanzas 17, 18, 25

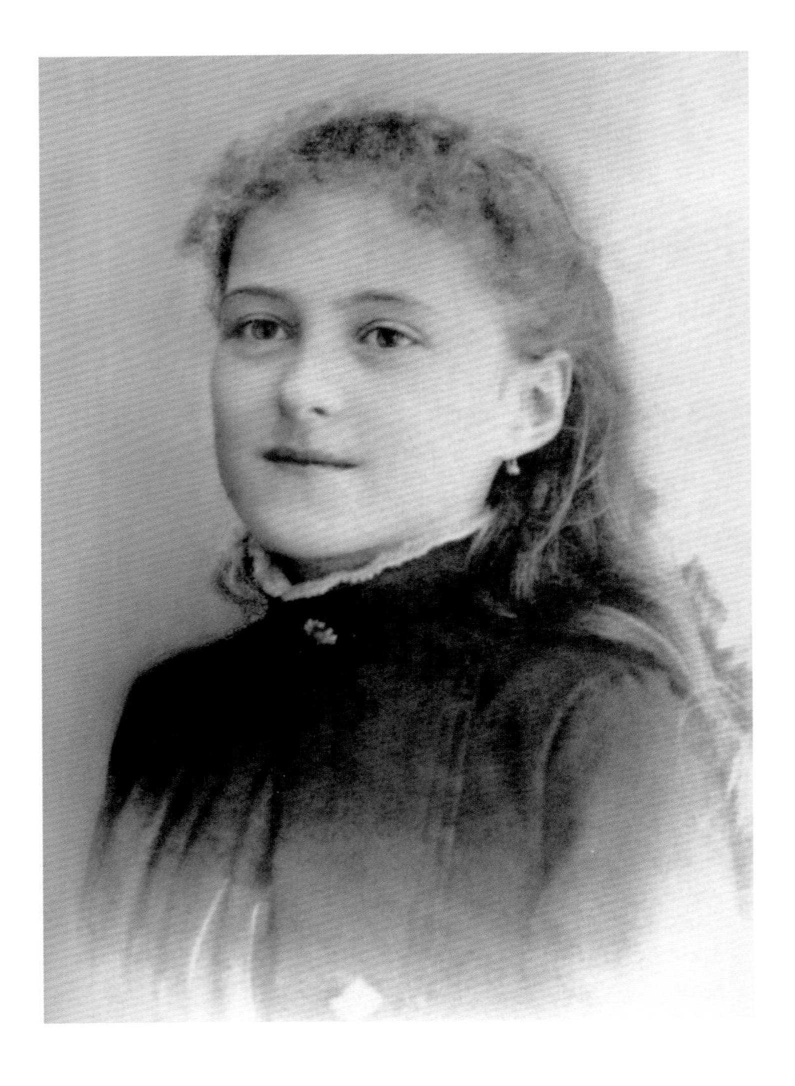

Conversion

On that night of light began the third period of my life, the most beautiful and the most filled with graces from heaven. The work I had been unable to do in ten years was done by Jesus in one instant, contenting himself with my good will which was never lacking. I could say to Him like His apostles: "Master, I fished all night and caught nothing." More merciful to me than He was to His disciples, Jesus took the net Himself, cast it, and drew it in filled with fish. He made me a fisher of souls. I experienced a great desire to work for the conversion of sinners, a desire I hadn't felt so intensely before. I felt charity enter into my soul, and the need to forget myself and to please others; since then I've been happy!

MS A 45 vo

Lord Jesus,

Fill our hearts with your divine charity so that we may learn to practise fraternal charity towards all those we meet. Teach us how to forget ourselves and to seek to serve others. With Thérèse, and full of confidence in your mercy for sinners, we pray to you: grant us the grace of conversion so that we too might become apostles of mercy in your service.

Amen.

At 15, Thérèse tells her father of her vocation and asks him for permission to enter Carmel. Statue in the garden of Les Buissonnets, Lisieux.

Vocation

I was to pass through many trials but the divine call was so strong that had I been forced to pass through flames, I would have done it out of love for Jesus.

MS A 49 ro

How beautiful is the vocation which has as its aim the preservation of the salt destined for souls! This is Carmel's vocation since the sole purpose of our prayers and sacrifices is to be the apostle of the apostles. We are to pray for them while they are preaching to souls through their words and especially their example.

MS A 56 ro

O Heart of Jesus, treasure of tenderness,
You Yourself are my happiness, my only hope.
You who knew how to charm my tender youth,
Stay near me till the last night.
Lord, to you alone I've given my life,
And all my desires are well-known to you.
It's in your ever-infinite goodness
That I want to lose myself, O Heart of Jesus!

Poem 23 stanza 6

Thirst for souls

One Sunday, looking at a picture of Our Lord on the Cross, I was struck by the blood flowing from one of the divine hands. I felt a great pang of sorrow when thinking this blood was falling to the ground without anyone's hastening to gather it up. I was resolved to remain in spirit at the foot of the Cross and to receive the divine dew. I understood I was then to pour it out upon souls. The cry of Jesus on the Cross sounded continually in my heart: "I thirst!" These words ignited within me an unknown and very living fire. I wanted to give my Beloved to drink and I felt myself consumed with a thirst for souls. As yet, it was not the souls of priests that attracted me, but those of great sinners; I burned with the desire to snatch them from the eternal flames.

MS A 45 vo

O Little Saint,

now that you see the crucified Jesus in heaven still bearing the wounds caused by sin, you know still more clearly than you did upon earth the value of souls, and the priceless worth of that Precious Blood, which He shed to save them. As children for whom Christ died, obtain for us all the graces we need in order to profit by His Precious Blood. May we too show to others the compassion He pours out upon us, so that they also may find true peace in Him.

Amen.

The church of the Carmel in Lisieux.

*“ O Saint Mary Magdalene!
obtain for me the grace that my life
may be one act of love. ”*

A hidden treasure

Jesus is a *hidden* treasure, an inestimable good which few souls can find, for it is *hidden*, and the world loves what sparkles. Ah! if Jesus had willed to show Himself to all souls with His ineffable gifts, no doubt there is not one of them that would have despised Him. However, He does not will that we love Him for His gifts, *He Himself* must be our *reward*. To find a hidden thing one must hide oneself; our life must then be a *mystery*. We must be like Jesus, Jesus whose *face was hidden*.

LT 145

Dear Saint Thérèse,

the beloved flower of Jesus and Mary, the Immaculate Virgin, who specially favoured you, even from your infancy, so as to lead you to her cloister and there to conduct you as a spouse of God up to the Altar; obtain for me, O little Saint, that Mary would continue to shower her blessing upon me, so that I may ever remain her faithful servant, ever loving her and imitating her virtues, especially the virtue of the ardent love of God.

Amen.

1877.

Jesus teaches without the noise of words

But it is especially the Gospels that sustain me during my hours of prayer, for in them I find what is necessary for my poor little soul. I am constantly discovering in them new lights, hidden and mysterious meanings. I understand and I know from experience that: "The kingdom of God is within you." Jesus has no need of books or teachers to instruct souls; He teaches without the noise of words. Never have I heard Him speak, but I feel that He is within me at each moment; He is guiding and inspiring me with what I must say and do. I find just when I need them certain lights that I had not seen until then, and it isn't most frequently during my hours of prayer that these are most abundant but rather in the midst of my daily occupations.

MS A 83 vo

O Little Flower of Jesus,
from the very first moment of your religious life you thought only of denying yourself in all things so as to follow Jesus perfectly; help me to bear patiently the trials of my daily life. Teach me to make use of the trials, the sufferings, the humiliations, that come my way, to learn to know myself better and to love God more.

Amen.

"*Jesus, my only Love, how I love to strew Flowers*
Each evening at the foot of your Crucifix!
In unpetalling the springtime rose for you,
I would like to dry your tears."

Charity

Ah! Lord, I know you don't command the impossible. You know better than I do my weakness and imperfection; You know very well that never would I be able to love my Sisters as You love them, unless You, O my Jesus, loved them in me. It is because You wanted to give me this grace that You made Your new commandment. Oh! How I love this new commandment since it gives me the assurance that Your Will is to love in me all those You command me to love!

Yes, I feel it, when I am charitable, it is Jesus alone who is acting in me, and the more united I am to Him, the more also do I love my Sisters.

MS C 12 vo

Divine Jesus, listen to my prayer.
By my love I want to make you rejoice.
You know well, I want to please you alone.
Deign to grant my most ardent desire.
I accept the trials of this sad exile
To delight you and to console your heart.
But change all my works into love,
O my Spouse, my Beloved Saviour.

Poem 41 stanza 1

Born for Glory

I considered that I was born for glory and when I searched out the means of attaining it, [God] made me understand my own glory would not be evident to the eyes of mortals, that it would consist in becoming a great saint! This desire would certainly appear daring if one were to consider how weak and imperfect I was, and how, after seven years in the religious life, I still am weak and imperfect. I always feel, however, the same bold confidence of becoming a great saint because I don't count on my merits, since I have none, but I trust in Him who is Virtue and Holiness. God alone, content with my weak efforts will raise me to Himself and make me a saint.

MS A 32 ro

O God, who in your mercy raised Thérèse to yourself and made her a great saint, grant us through her intercession to be confident like her in your goodness as our Father, and make us reach the perfection to which you call us. Through fidelity in the small tasks of everyday life, animated by the love of Christ, and nourished by the Church, may we achieve true holiness.

Amen.

The power of Prayer

How great is the power of Prayer! One could call it a Queen who has at each instant free access to the King and who is able to obtain whatever she asks. To be heard it is not necessary to read from a book some beautiful formula composed for the occasion. If this were the case, alas, I would have to be pitied! Outside the Divine Office which I am very unworthy to recite, I do not have the courage to force myself to search out beautiful prayers in books. There are so many of them it really gives me a headache! and each prayer is more beautiful than the others. I cannot recite them all and not knowing which to choose, I do like children who do not know how to read, I say very simply to God what I wish to say, without composing beautiful sentences, and He always understands me. For me, prayer is an aspiration of the heart, it is a simple glance directed to heaven, it is a cry of gratitude and love in the midst of trial as well as joy; finally, it is something great, supernatural, which expands my soul and unites me to Jesus.

MS C 25 ro/vo

Saint Thérèse,
Show us the way of silent prayer as you practised it, in a simple conversation with God present within us. Grant us to have faith in the power of prayer and to persevere in this sharing heart to heart with God who loves us.

Amen.

Thérèse's writing desk and one of her manuscripts.

“Jesus, gentle and humble of Heart, make my heart like yours!”

Daily Offering

My God, I offer you all that I do today
for the intentions and the glory
of the Sacred Heart of Jesus.
I want to sanctify every beat of my heart,
my thoughts and my simplest works
by uniting them to his infinite merits.
I want to repair for my faults
by casting them into the furnace of his merciful love.

O my God!
I ask you for myself and for those dear to me
the grace to fulfil perfectly your holy will
and to accept for love of you
the joys and sorrows of this passing life
so that one day we may be reunited in Heaven
for all eternity,

Amen.

Prayer 10

Dear Father, I offer you all my weakness and
frailties, this day and every day.
My Jesus, turn your heart towards those who
suffer, and bring them comfort.
O Holy Spirit, if it is in accordance with the Father's
will, grant the graces of healing to those who are sick,
through the merits and intercession of Saint Thérèse.

Amen.

“ My God, I believe in you,
I hope in you,
I love you with all my heart. ”

Lifting the world

All the saints have understood this, and more especially those who filled the world with the light of the Gospel teachings. Was it not in prayer that St Paul, St Augustine, St John of the Cross, St Thomas Aquinas, St Francis, St Dominic, and so many other famous Friends of God have drawn out this divine science which delights the greatest geniuses? A scholar has said: "*Give me a lever and a fulcrum and I will lift the world.*" What Archimedes was not able to obtain, for his request was not directed by God and was only made from a material viewpoint, the saints have obtained in all its fullness. The Almighty has given them as fulcrum: Himself alone; as lever: prayer which burns with a fire of love. And it is in this way that they have lifted the world; it is in this way that the saints still militant lift it, and that, until the end of time, the saints to come will lift it.

MS C 36 ro/vo

O God our Father, you have promised your kingdom to those who are willing to become like little children. Help us to follow the way of Saint Thérèse with confidence so that by her prayers we may come to know your eternal glory. Grant this through our Lord Jesus Christ, your Son, who lives and reigns with you and the Holy Spirit, one God, for ever and ever.

Amen.

My vocation is Love

Considering the mystical body of the Church, I had not recognised myself in any of the members described by St Paul, or rather I desired to see myself in them all. Charity gave me the key to my vocation. I understood that if the Church had a body composed of different members, the most necessary and most noble of all could not be lacking to it, and so I understood that the Church had a Heart and that this Heart was burning with Love. I understood it was Love alone that made the Church's members act, that if Love ever became extinct, apostles would not preach the Gospel and martyrs would not shed their blood. I understood that Love comprised all vocations, that Love was everything, that it embraced all times and places ... in a word, that it was eternal!

Then in the excess of my delirious joy, I cried out: O Jesus, my Love, my vocation, at last I have found it ... my vocation is Love!

Yes, I have found my place in the Church and it is You, O my God, who have given me this place; in the heart of the Church, my Mother, I shall be Love.

MS B 3 vo

O little Martyr of Love you know now even better than in the days of your pilgrimage that love embraces all vocations: that it is love alone that counts, which unites us perfectly with God and conforms our will with His. All you sought on earth was love; to love Jesus as He had never yet been loved. Use your power in heaven to make us love Him. If only we love Him we shall desire to make Him loved by others; we shall pray much for souls. We shall no longer fear death, for it will unite us with Him for ever. Obtain for us the grace to do all for the love of God, to give Him pleasure, to love Him so well that He may be pleased with us as He was with you.

Amen.

A chasuble painted by St Thérèse of the Child Jesus and the Holy Face. The lilies represent her family, the closed lilies representing her brothers and sisters who had died.

Prayer to the Holy Face

O Adorable Face of Jesus,
the only Beauty that captivates my heart,
deign to imprint in me your Divine Likeness
so that you may not behold the soul of your little bride
without seeing Yourself in her.

O my Beloved,
for love of you, I accept not seeing here below
the gentleness of your Look
nor feeling the ineffable kiss of your Mouth,
but I beg you to inflame me with your love
so that it may consume me rapidly
and soon bring me into your presence.

Prayer 16

Jesus, Who in Your bitter Passion,
became the reproach of men
and the Man of Sorrows,
I venerate Your Holy Face
on which shone the beauty and gentleness of Divinity.
In those disfigured features,
I recognise Your infinite Love,
and I long to love You,
and make You loved.
May I behold Your Glorious Face in Heaven.

Amen.

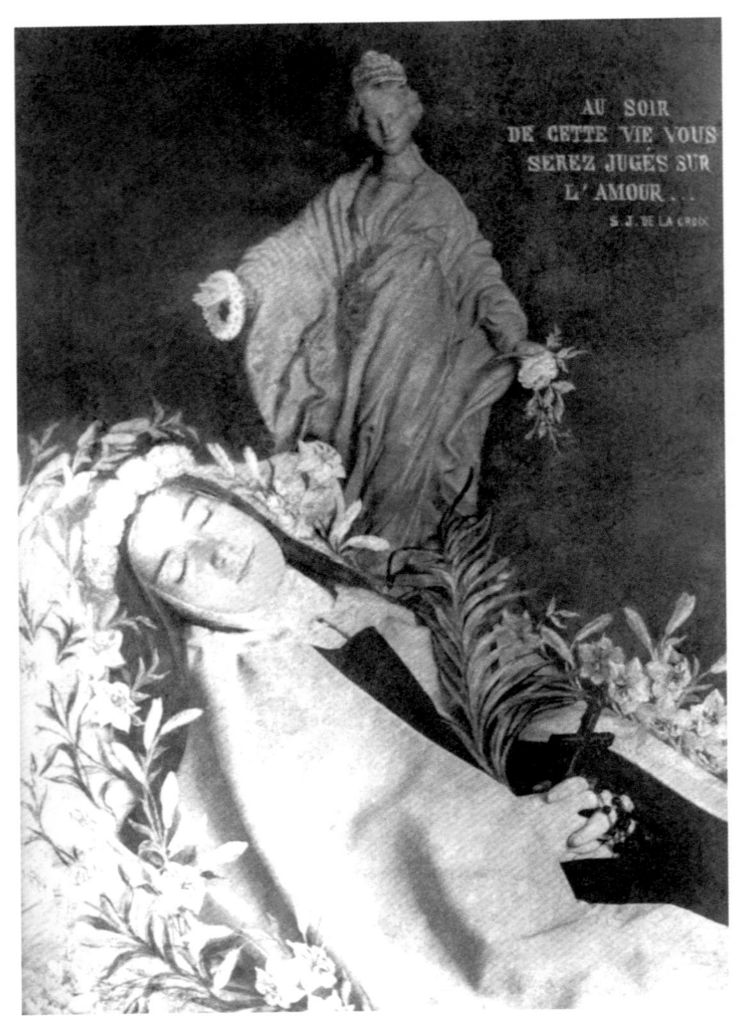

Thérèse on her deathbed.

My Mission

I feel especially that my mission is about to begin, my mission of making God loved as I love Him, of giving my little way to souls. If God answers my desires, my heaven will be spent on earth until the end of the world. Yes, I want to spend my heaven in doing good on earth.

Last Conversations
17 July 1897

Everything I have, everything I merit is for the Church and for souls.

Last Conversations
12 July 1897

Remember, O most gracious Little Flower your promise of never leaving any request made to you without an answer and of coming down to earth to do good. Full of confidence in your power with the Sacred Heart we implore your intercession in our need and beg of you to obtain the favour that we so urgently request if such be God's Holy Will.

Amen.

Wax effigy of Saint Thérèse in the church of the Carmel in Lisieux.

Prayer to Saint Thérèse for a holy death

Divine Saviour, at the end of my life
Come get me without the shadow of a delay.
Ah! show me your infinite tenderness
And the sweetness of your divine gaze.
With love, oh! may your voice call me,
Saying: Come, all is forgiven.
Come rest on my heart, my faithful spouse,
You have greatly loved me.

Poem 41 stanza 3

Dear Saint Thérèse,
like you, I have to die one day.
I beseech you, obtain from God, by reminding Him of your own precious death, that I may have a holy death, strengthened by the Sacraments of the Church, entirely resigned to the most holy will of God, and burning with love for Him.
May my last words on earth be
"My God, I love You."

Amen.

Procession of the relics of St Thérèse outside the Basilica in Lisieux.

" *O Jesus! grant me the grace in all I do to please You alone.* "

The way to perfection

At times, when I am reading certain spiritual treatises in which perfection is shown through a thousand obstacles, surrounded by a crowd of illusions, my poor little mind quickly tires; I close the learned book that is breaking my head and drying up my heart, and I take up Holy Scripture. Then all seems luminous to me, a single word uncovers for my soul infinite horizons, perfection seems simple to me. I see it is sufficient to recognise one's nothingness and to abandon oneself as a child into God's arms.

LT 226

Lord Jesus, through the life of St Thérèse, you have brought new hope to all who long to open their hearts to you. Teach us the secret of her 'Little Way' and help us to realise that we can always talk with You and bring You our gratitude, our difficulties and concerns.

Stay with us, Jesus, so that in the midst of our busy hours, we may turn to You in loving trust. Transform each passing moment of time into a moment of prayer. Fill every troubled heart with the confident faith of St Thérèse. In joy and in sorrow, in every circumstance, may our hearts rest in Your peace.

Amen.

Mosaic inside the Basilica in Lisieux.

With confidence and love

Yes, I feel it; even though I had on my conscience all the sins that can be committed, I would go, my heart broken with sorrow, and throw myself into Jesus' arms, for I know how much He loves the prodigal child who returns to Him. It is not because God, in His anticipating Mercy, has preserved my soul from mortal sin that I go to Him with confidence and love.

MS C 36 vo/37 ro

Thérèse,

Teach us how to open our hearts without reserve to the Holy Spirit as you did, to seek and find God's will in all the crises and choices, in the joys and disappointments, of our lives.

Gain for us too the grace to do His will with courage and untroubled hearts so that we may radiate a joy and a gladness like yours in the service of Our Lord.

May we, like you, work to build up the body of Christ throughout the world, so that the lost sheep may experience the mercy of God and return to the Father's embrace.

Amen.

“ Strewing Flowers, repeating your praise,
That is my only delight in this valley of tears.
Soon I shall go to Heaven with the little angels
To strew Flowers! ”

Not remaining inactive in heaven

Ah! Brother, I feel it, I shall be more useful to you in heaven than on earth, and it is with joy that I come to announce to you my coming entrance into that blessed city, sure that you will share my joy and will thank the Lord for giving me the means of helping you more effectively in your apostolic works. I really count on not remaining inactive in heaven. My desire is to work still for the Church and for souls. I am asking God for this and I am certain He will answer me.

Last Letter to Fr Roulland, her spiritual brother

O Saint Thérèse, Patroness of the Missions,
be a great missionary throughout the world to the end of time, remind our Master of His words: "The harvest is great, but the labourers few." Your zeal for souls was so great, obtain a like zeal for those now working for souls, and beg God to multiply their numbers, that the millions to whom Jesus is yet unknown, may be brought to know, love and follow Him.

Amen.

One of the reliquaries containing relics of St Thérèse during a visit to a parish.

The table of sinners

Lord, your child has understood your divine light, and she begs pardon for her brothers. She is resigned to eat the bread of sorrow as long as you desire it; she does not wish to rise up from this table filled with bitterness at which poor sinners are eating until the day set by you. Can she not say in her name and in the name of her brothers, "Have pity on us, O Lord, for we are poor sinners!" Oh! Lord, send us away justified. May all those who were not enlightened by the bright flame of faith one day see it shine. O Jesus! if it is needful that the table soiled by them be purified by a soul who loves you, then I desire to eat this bread of trial at this table until it pleases you to bring me into your bright kingdom.

MS C 6 ro

Eternal Father,
since you have given me for my inheritance
the Adorable Face of your Divine Son,
I offer it to you and I ask you,
in exchange for this infinitely precious Coin,
to forget the ingratitude of souls who are consecrated
to you and to pardon poor sinners.

Amen.

Prayer 15

Visit of the relics of St Thérèse to Lebanon in 2002.

“ O my God, look at the Face of Jesus and count all sinners among the elect. ”

I would like to travel over the whole earth

Ah! in spite of my littleness, I would like to enlighten souls as did the Prophets and the Doctors. I have the vocation of the Apostle. I would like to travel over the whole earth to preach Your Name and to plant Your glorious Cross on infidel soil. But O my Beloved, one mission alone would not be sufficient for me, I would want to preach the Gospel on all five continents simultaneously and even to the most remote isles. I would be a missionary, not for a few years only but from the beginning of creation until the consummation of the ages.

MS B 3 ro

O Lord,

You inspired in Thérèse a burning desire for evangelisation throughout the world. You have fulfilled her desires beyond death and allow her to do good through the visits of her relics to the various peoples of the earth and even to remote islands. We entrust to you the spiritual fruitfulness of her visit to this country. May the presence of her relics draw more people to know Your name and to welcome the message of the Gospel.

Amen.

Veneration of the relics of St Thérèse in Latvia in 2007.

“ My God, I love you with all my heart. ”

Novena to Saint Thérèse in honour of the Holy Trinity

The *Glory be to the Father* praising the Holy Trinity is said twenty-five times each of the nine days, in thanksgiving for all the blessings and favours given to St Thérèse of the Child Jesus during the twenty-five years of her life. In addition, this or a similar prayer may be used:

Holy Trinity, God the Father, God the Son and God the Holy Spirit, I thank Thee for all the blessings and favours Thou hast showered upon the soul of Thy servant Thérèse of the Child Jesus, during the twenty-five years she spent here on earth, and in consideration of the merits of this Thy most beloved Saint, I beseech Thee to grant me this favour, if it is in accordance with Thy most Holy Will and is not an obstacle to my salvation.

After this prayer, the twenty-five *Glory bes* are said; between each of these this short prayer may be included:

St Thérèse of the Child Jesus, pray for us.

Novena of Prayer through the Intercession of Saint Thérèse of the Child Jesus

God our Father,
You welcome near You those who serve You faithfully in this world: we invoke Saint Thérèse of the Child Jesus because of her love for You. Her childlike trust made her hope "that You would do her will in Heaven because she had always done yours on earth." I beg You to grant the prayer I make to You in faith as I entrust myself to her intercession.

Our Father

Lord Jesus,
only Son of God and our Saviour, remember that Saint Thérèse of the Child Jesus spent her life here below for the salvation of souls and wanted "to spend her Heaven doing good on earth." Because she was your beloved spouse and was impassioned for your glory, we pray to her. I depend on You to grant the graces I implore through her intercession.

Hail Mary

Holy Spirit,
source of all grace and all love, it is through your action that Saint Thérèse of the Child Jesus was so filled with divine attentions and responded to them with such perfect fidelity. Since she intercedes for us now and wants no rest until the end of time, we pray through her. I ask You to inspire and to hear my prayer, so that there may be granted to me the favour entrusted to her intercession.

Glory be to the Father

O Saint Thérèse of the Child Jesus,
see what confidence I have in you, and welcome my intentions. Intercede for me with the Blessed Virgin Mary, who came to smile on you when you were suffering. Look on all those undergoing distress and trials and also on all those who pray to you: I unite myself to them as my brothers and sisters. Through the graces we desire, if it be the Lord's will, make us stronger in Faith, Hope and Love on the road to life. May we be assisted at the moment of death so that we may pass from this world into the peace of the Father and know the eternal joy of the children of God.

Amen.

Act of Oblation to Merciful Love

Offering of myself as a Victim of Holocaust
to God's Merciful Love

O My God! Most Blessed Trinity, I desire to Love you and make you Loved, to work for the glory of Holy Church by saving souls on earth and liberating those suffering in purgatory. I desire to accomplish your will perfectly and to reach the degree of glory you have prepared for me in your kingdom. I desire, in a word, to be a Saint, but I feel my helplessness and I beg you, O my God! to be yourself my Sanctity!

Since You loved me so much as to give me your only Son as my Saviour and my Spouse, the infinite treasures of his merits are mine. I offer them to you with gladness, begging you to look on me only through the Face of Jesus and in his Heart burning with Love.

I offer you, too, all the merits of the Saints (in Heaven and on earth), their acts of Love, and those of the Holy Angels. Finally, I offer you, O Blessed Trinity! the Love and merits of the Blessed Virgin, my dear Mother. It is to her I abandon my offering, begging her to present it to you. Her Divine Son, my Beloved Spouse, told us in the days of his mortal life: "Whatsoever you ask the Father in my name he will give it to you!" I am certain, then, that you will grant my desires; I know, O my God! that the more you want to give, the more you make us desire. I feel in my heart immense desires and it is with confidence I ask you to come and take possession of my soul. Ah! I cannot receive Holy Communion as often as I desire, but, Lord, are you not All-Powerful? Remain in me as in a tabernacle and never separate yourself from your little host.

I want to console you for the ingratitude of the wicked, and I beg of you to take away my freedom to displease you. If through weakness I sometimes fall, may your Divine Glance cleanse my soul immediately, consuming all my imperfections like the fire that transforms everything into itself.

I thank you, O my God! for all the graces you have granted me, especially the grace of making me pass through the crucible of suffering. It is with joy I shall contemplate You on the last day carrying the sceptre of your Cross. Since you deigned to give me a share in this very precious Cross, I hope in Heaven to resemble you and to see shining in my glorified body the sacred stigmata of Your Passion.

After earth's exile, I hope to go and enjoy you in the Fatherland, but I do not want to lay up merits for Heaven. I want to work for your Love alone with the one purpose of pleasing you, consoling your Sacred Heart, and saving souls who will love you eternally.

In the evening of this life, I shall appear before you with empty hands, for I do not ask you, Lord, to count my works. All our justice is stained in your eyes. I wish, then, to be clothed in your own Justice and to receive from your Love the eternal possession of Yourself. I want no other Throne, no other Crown but You, my Beloved!

Time is nothing in your eyes, and a single day is like a thousand years; you can, then, in one instant prepare me to appear before you.

In order to live in one single act of perfect Love, I offer myself as a victim of holocaust to your merciful love, asking you to consume me incessantly, allowing the waves of infinite tenderness shut up within you to overflow into my soul, and that thus I may become a Martyr of your Love, O my God!

May this martyrdom, after having prepared me to appear before you, finally cause me to die and may my soul take its flight without any delay into the eternal embrace of Your Merciful Love.

I want, O my Beloved, at each beat of my heart to renew this offering to you an infinite number of times, until the shadows having disappeared I may be able to tell you of my Love in an Eternal Face to Face!

Marie-Françoise-Thérèse of the Child Jesus
and the Holy Face
unworthy Carmelite religious

Prayer 6

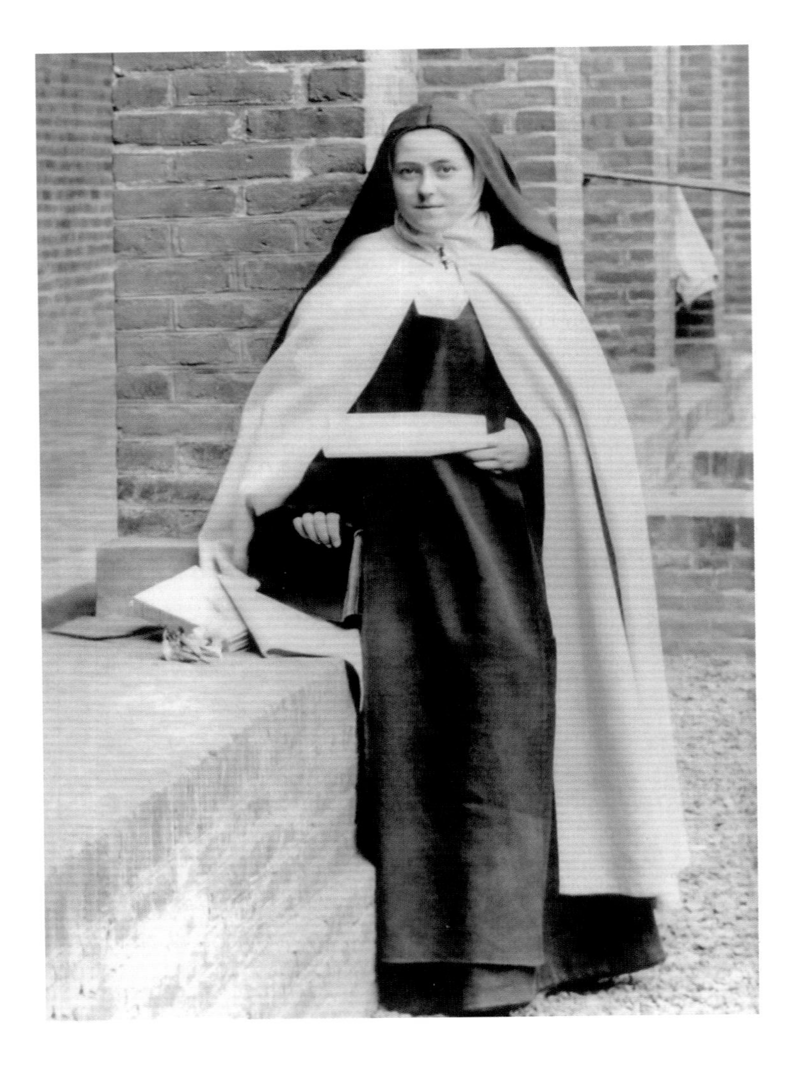

Litany of Saint Thérèse of the Child Jesus and the Holy Face

Lord, have mercy. *Lord, have mercy.*
Christ, have mercy. *Christ, have mercy.*
Lord, have mercy. *Lord, have mercy.*

Christ, hear us. *Christ, graciously hear us.*
God, the Father in Heaven, *have mercy on us.*
God, the Son, Redeemer of the world, *have mercy on us.*
God the Holy Spirit, *have mercy on us.*
Holy Trinity, one God, *have mercy on us.*

Holy Mary, Mother of God, *pray for us.*
St Joseph, *pray for us.*
St Teresa of Jesus, *pray for us.*
St John of the Cross, *pray for us.*
St Thérèse of the Child Jesus and the Holy Face, *pray for us.*
St Thérèse, Gift of God to Carmel, *pray for us.*
St Thérèse, Gift of God to the Church, *pray for us.*
St Thérèse, Doctor of the Universal Church, *pray for us.*
St Thérèse, Patroness of the Missions, *pray for us.*
St Thérèse, beloved child of the heavenly Father, *pray for us.*
St Thérèse, passionately in love with Jesus, *pray for us.*
St Thérèse, who so wanted to resemble the Child Jesus, *pray for us.*
St Thérèse, who so wanted to resemble the suffering of Jesus, *pray for us.*
St Thérèse, on fire with love through the Holy Spirit, *pray for us.*
St Thérèse, who gave us the 'little way of spiritual childhood', *pray for us.*
St Thérèse, who only sought the truth, *pray for us.*
St Thérèse, who 'chose all' that God wanted, *pray for us.*
St Thérèse, who understood and practised humility of heart, *pray for us.*

St Thérèse, who forgot yourself to make others happy, *pray for us.*
St Thérèse, who fought with the weapons of prayer and sacrifice, *pray for us.*
St Thérèse, who wanted to love like Jesus Himself, *pray for us.*
St Thérèse, who understood and lived charity, *pray for us.*
St Thérèse, who praised the works of the Creator, *pray for us.*
St Thérèse, who praised the mercies of the Lord, *pray for us.*
St Thérèse, poor, chaste, and obedient, *pray for us.*
St Thérèse, faithful in the littlest things, *pray for us.*
St Thérèse, whose weakness is folly, *pray for us.*
St Thérèse, free and joyful, *pray for us.*
St Thérèse, patient and courageous, *pray for us.*
St Thérèse, simple in joy and suffering, *pray for us.*
St Thérèse, tried in your faith, *pray for us.*
St Thérèse, who hoped against all hope, *pray for us.*
St Thérèse, who refused God nothing, *pray for us.*
St Thérèse, rapidly consumed by Love, *pray for us.*
St Thérèse, martyr of Love, *pray for us.*
St Thérèse, nourished by the Word of God, *pray for us.*
St Thérèse, burning with desire for the Eucharist, *pray for us.*
St Thérèse, love in the heart of the Church, *pray for us.*
St Thérèse, word of God for the world, *pray for us.*
St Thérèse, teacher of the spiritual life, *pray for us.*
St Thérèse, apostle of Mercy, *pray for us.*
St Thérèse, offered to Merciful Love, *pray for us.*
St Thérèse, who came before God with empty hands, *pray for us.*
St Thérèse, happy in your weakness, *pray for us.*
St Thérèse, trusting in spite of everything, *pray for us.*
St Thérèse, who found in abandonment to the Father an ocean of peace, *pray for us.*
St Thérèse, consumed with zeal for the salvation of souls, *pray for us.*
St Thérèse, sister and friend of priests, *pray for us.*

St Thérèse, support of your brother missionaries, *pray for us.*
St Thérèse, mother of a multitude, *pray for us.*
St Thérèse, everyone's sister, *pray for us.*
St Thérèse, seated at the table of sinners, *pray for us.*
St Thérèse, who made a condemned criminal your first child, *pray for us.*
St Thérèse, close to prisoners, sister of the wounded in life, *pray for us.*
St Thérèse, friend of unbelievers, *pray for us.*
St Thérèse, close to those who are tempted and who doubt, *pray for us.*
St Thérèse, close to those who despair, *pray for us.*
St Thérèse, presence of pardon and peace, *pray for us.*
St Thérèse, witness of God, our Merciful Father, *pray for us.*
St Thérèse, witness of Christ, Servant and Saviour, *pray for us.*
St Thérèse, witness of the Spirit of Love and Holiness, *pray for us.*

Lamb of God, you take away the sins of the world. *Spare us, O Lord.*
Lamb of God, you take away the sins of the world. *Graciously hear us, O Lord.*
Lamb of God, you take away the sins of the world. *Have mercy on us.*

Pray for us, St Thérèse, *that we may be made worthy of the promises of Christ.*

Let us pray.
God our Father, You have promised your Kingdom to those who are willing to become like little children. Help us to follow the way of Saint Thérèse with confidence so that by her prayers we may come to know your eternal glory. Through Christ our Lord.

Amen.

Acknowledgements

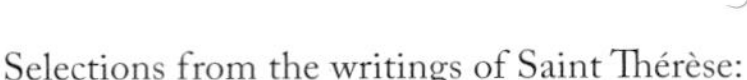

Selections from the writings of Saint Thérèse:

Story of a Soul: The Autobiography of St. Thérèse of Lisieux, translated by John Clarke, OCD (Washington DC, 1975), © 1975 by the Washington Province of Discalced Carmelites, ICS Publications, 2131 Lincoln Road NE, Washington, DC 20002, USA.

St. Thérèse of Lisieux: Her Last Conversations, translated by John Clarke, OCD (Washington DC, 1977), © 1977 by the Washington Province of Discalced Carmelites, ICS Publications.

General correspondence, vol. 2, translated by John Clarke, OCD (Washington DC, 1988), © 1988 by the Washington Province of Discalced Carmelites, ICS Publications.

The Poetry of St. Thérèse of Lisieux, translated by Donald Kinney, OCD (Washington DC, 1996), © 1996 by the Washington Province of Discalced Carmelites, ICS Publications.

The Prayers of St. Thérèse of Lisieux, translated by Aletheia Kane, OCD (Washington DC, 1997), © 1997 by the Washington Province of Discalced Carmelites, ICS Publications.

Pictures of Saint Thérèse: © Office Central de Lisieux.

Other pictures: © Pèlerinage de Lisieux.
The publishers are grateful to Louis-Vincent Lejeune for his kind assistance.

Papal texts on pages 4, 6-7: © Libreria Editrice Vaticana.

“ After my death I will send a shower of roses upon the earth. ”